HEART EXPRESSIONS

BY

JAN MARTEN

HEART EXPRESSIONS TO AID YOU IN EXPLORING
YOUR OWN EXPRESSIONS

DEDICATION

TO MY SPIRIT FRIENDS

INTRODUCTION

This book was conceived and born in thirty days. I had no intention of writing such a book. I was writing about how past lives affect present ones. One day, without any thought of what I was doing, I picked up a pen and notebook, and began writing. This book was the amazing result. Each of "The Expressions" flowed out of me without any effort.

Was this book channeled? I don't feel that it was. However, I am very sure that I had help. Other Side help. I would pick up the pen with no idea of what I wanted to say and the words were given to me one by one.

My heart overflows with gratitude to my Spirit Friends for their wisdom and inspiration. It is so comforting to know that they are always here loving and guiding us.

The Expressions here are my truths. **I KNOW** them to be true. I hope that they will be true for you also. Explore them and find out. Go within your own heart and become aware of what is there.

It is my sincere wish that this book would instill a strong desire in you to learn more, feel more, read more, and study more.

There is nothing more rewarding than the walk along the spiritual path.

Peace, Love, Light & Life,

Jan Marten

HOW TO USE THIS BOOK

This book is meant to be absorbed in small bites, not one or two big gulps. Read one Expression at a time, see what feelings and thoughts it brings forth. After making sure of your feelings, take the appropriate action.

You can read the book from the beginning in sequence or you can skip around. Hold the book over your heart for a minute or two, ask for guidance, then let it fall open where it will. Our Spirit Friends have a way of guiding us to the lesson that we most need to learn at the time.

Another way to use the book is to look at the Table of Contents and see if you are drawn to any particular title. You can also close your eyes and run your finger over the Table of Contents. Read the Expression where your finger stops.

You will notice, that some titles are the same but are numbered 2, 3 or 4.

These can be read one at a time or taken as a whole. Whatever you feel drawn to do.

As always, YOU ARE IN CONTROL, it is your choice.

The empty space between the Expression and the affirmation is YOUR space. Use it as you will. Write down your thoughts and feelings or draw pictures of how you feel. Use crayons, or colored pencils or whatever is handy at the time.

MAKE THIS BOOK YOURS!

Do not fear any of the emotions that are stirred up, please KNOW that they are a necessary part of your spiritual growth. Flow with them and don't put any pressure on yourself.

May this book be the first step to a new, more joyous, more fulfilling life.

TABLE OF CONTENTS

THERE IS NOTHING IN THE UNIVERSE TO FEAR

There is nothing, ever, in any way, that can harm your soul. Your soul is eternal. You will shed the coat that is your outward body and, after a time of reflection, put on another body to resume your learning process. The body is only a tool to help you learn. When you finish with it, you choose a different one to help you overcome your fears and to help you realize that there is absolutely nothing in the universe to fear.

THERE IS ONLY LOVE.

I realize that there is nothing in the universe to fear.

INNER PEACE

Inner peace is possible no matter what your outward circumstances. Inner peace comes from knowing without a doubt that we live forever and that we are here on this Earth plane only to learn. We know that we will survive the situations in our lives that cause us pain. We also know that we are love and love is all there is. Knowing these things, we are able to bring this inner peace into the outward circumstances of our lives.

Today I let others see my inner peace.

KNOWERS

Be a knower, not a believer. Say: **I KNOW**. Ask for the understanding and listen to the feelings within you. Trust the wisdom of your feelings.

You don't have to try hard, just let the "knowing" come. It is there and you will soon realize it. The intent to know is enough.

You do not have to convince yourself of anything. Your soul knows all things. Be aware of this in your conscious mind.

Today I feel the knowing inside of me.

IT'S ALL RIGHT

No matter what you feel is not working in your life, it's all right. If you can accept these three words your life will be much more loving and balanced. If you trust your own wisdom you will know the truth of these words.

IT'S ALL RIGHT. It truly is.

KNOW this in the essence of your being. Whatever happens, it's all right.

Today I know that whatever happens, it's all right.

UNIVERSAL TRUTH

Every soul on every plane is connected to each other within the higher self. We are all a part of a great energy which we call GOD. Because we are a Part of GOD, WE ARE GOD. Nothing we can ever do will change this fact. We are energy and energy creates continuously.

Today I recognize my connection to God.

ACCEPTANCE

Accept yourself EXACTLY as you are right now.
Go on, do it. Take a deep breath, let it out slowly, then
say out loud, "I accept myself just as I am."

What kind of feelings does this stir up in you?
Examine them carefully. Do you immediately deny it? Why?
You can't have self-love unless you have acceptance.
Appreciate and support yourself exactly as you are right now.

"I accept myself just as I am."

FOREVER

YOU ARE FOREVER.

JOY

Each of us has a right to experience joy. Give yourself permission to be joyful. Stop doing everything that you don't enjoy. Is it hard to do? Think about it very carefully. Find the things in your life that you don't enjoy and eliminate them one by one. Soon you will find yourself looking forward to every moment and the joy it brings.

Start right now by putting a joyful smile on your face and allowing it to fill your heart.

Today I exchange one thing that I don't enjoy doing for one that I do.

YOU ARE LIGHT

The light is within you. Imagine a light inside your body, feel its warmth, its love. As you become more aware of it, feel it grow and fill you up. Allow it to flow to those around you. Everyone you meet is touched by the light within you. **KNOW** that you are light. Let your light take away all the darkness within and around you.

TODAY I LET MY LIGHT SHINE.

PURPOSE OF LIFE

THE PURPOSE OF LIFE IS TO LEARN, TO GROW, AND TO RETURN TO THE ONENESS, THAT IS ALL THERE IS.

APPRECIATION

We all enjoy being truthful with people who appreciate us.

Appreciation comes from the heart.

The more we appreciate, the more our heart opens.

There are many ways of expressing it to others.

We can **speak** words, we can **write** words, we can give gifts and we can send positive and loving thoughts.

The more you appreciate and give thanks for, the more increase of everything you receive in your own life.

Today I tell someone how much I appreciate them.

CELEBRATE LIFE

Life is a celebration, so CELEBRATE! Celebrate it with joy, wonder and thankfulness that you are alive to celebrate! Glorify life, it is an honor to be alive, to be a part of this wondrous experience we call life. Have fun with life, laugh with it and at it. Know that life is not meant to be a burden but a celebration.

Today I drink a toast to life!

HIGHER SELF

The higher self is the part of you that is connected to every other soul. It speaks to you in a still small voice and it tries to get your attention.

It doesn't intrude, you have the free will to accept or reject its help. It speaks to you through meditation and through your dreams.

Your desire to reach your higher self will enable you to do so.

KNOW that your higher self is Oneness.

I get in touch with my higher self.

BE SILENT

Quiet your mind. Practice it daily. Be still, sit quietly, breathe deeply and just be. Don't do anything, don't think of anything, be still and rest physically, mentally, emotionally and especially spiritually.

This way your soul will be able to speak more clearly to you.

The stillness of your mind will give you space for your ideas to enter.

Today I quiet my mind for ten minutes.

FAILURE

THERE IS NO SUCH THING AS FAILURE

Only stepping-stones on the way to success.

Today I resolve to never use the word FAILURE again.

UNLIMITED LOVE

The love of God is unlimited. It is so long, so wide, so, deep and so high that we will never see the end of it. It fills us up until we too become unlimited love.

God's unlimited love is always with us even when we don't recognize it.

Become aware of it, pay attention to your feelings, recognize that love and its source.

Today I seek the source of unlimited love.

ONENESS

WE ARE ALL ONE

JUDGMENTS

The word "JUDGMENT" implies an alternative. We do have more than one choice. We have the choice NOT to judge. Either others or ourselves. We can accept the emotion and experience into our essence without judgment and with unconditional love. Learn to let go of judgments and to accept what is.

Beginning today, I eliminate the word "judgment" from my vocabulary.

PEACE OF HEART

When you feel strong and in control of your life you are coming from your heart. You can't understand with your mind, only your heart. Your heart **KNOWS** that NO ONE ever means to hurt anyone else.

The heart knows only love.

Hurt comes from ignorance and fear. When there is no fear and no pain, when you feel only love, when you feel at one with everything,

THIS IS WHEN YOU HAVE PEACE OF HEART.

I have peace of heart.

THE SPIRITUAL PATH

Enjoy the walk along the path and forget that you are even on a path. Know that every step you take in whatever direction is a step along that path. Know also that everyone else is also walking the same path towards the same destination.

Walk the path with love for all things, including yourself.

I enjoy my walk along the path.

LISTEN WITH A QUIET MIND

When you listen to others, do so with a quiet mind. You can not hear them fully if your mind is busy with your own thoughts.

Quiet your mind and open your heart to hear what others have to say to you. Hear not only their words but the feelings underneath the words.

Respond with love.

I listen to others with a quiet mind.

DESIRE

Desire can bring us closer to wholeness or it can move us further away. Desire is necessary for us to fulfill our spiritual purpose. It is the desire to be complete that drives us. Anything that we want to change in our lives can be accomplished if the desire is there.

Today I recognize the importance of desire.

GENTLENESS

Treat everyone that you meet today, beginning with yourself, with the utmost gentleness. Each person is carrying a heavy load and needs gentleness from you. Be gentle in everything you say and do. Send each person positive thoughts filled with light. Let the love you feel in your soul come out and gently enfold others.

I am gentle with everyone today.

FEAR

Fear is the absence of love. Fear is a lack of understanding. Fear is like a background noise that affects everything that you do.

Each of us creates his own fears. Allow the knowledge that you create your own fears to enter you. Be receptive toward it and have the courage to face it . Then you will be well on your way to understanding your fear, accepting it and releasing it.

I AM SAFE

SEE THE BUTTERFLIES IN YOUR LIFE

You are walking along a busy street when suddenly a butterfly flies by. You turn and stare in delight, watching until it disappears from sight. Then you continue on your way with a smile on your face.

Butterflies are all around you. Little things that delight and refresh your heart. Become aware of them and their importance, A shared laugh, a bird's song, rainbow of colors sparkling off a crystal, an unexpected call from an absent friend. These are all butterflies that give you a lift and delight you.

Become aware of them.

I see butterflies today.

SOUL DEVELOPMENT

The most important thing in your life is the development of your soul. You may not recognize this to be so but your soul knows it to be the truth. We all desire to evolve spiritually, to let go of the emotions that cause fear and to learn to love unconditionally.

Today I take an active part in my soul's development.

ABUNDANCE

There is unlimited abundance all around us. There is plenty for everyone. We can learn to create exactly what we want by using our energy and thoughts. Do you know exactly what you want?

Spend some time with yourself deciding what you want. Make sure that it IS really what you want. Become aware that material possessions will not give you the feelings of love, peace and aliveness that you seek.

Use the power within you to create exactly what it is you desire.

I affirm this over and over: I KNOW WHAT I WANT AND I CREATE IT.

ENERGY

NOTHING CAN EVER DESTROY ENERGY.
IT CAN ONLY BE TRANSFORMED.

YOU ARE ENERGY.

CHANGING YOUR ATTITUDE

Is there someone in your life with whom you are having difficulty? Acknowledge that there is nothing you can do to change that person. Recognize that you CAN change your own attitude. Make a strong effort to do so, work at it. Every time you think of or see the person, imagine a white beam of light corning from you and send it to that person. Feel the connection between you. It is the light of love.

Today I send out the light of love.

LETTING GO

Sometimes we hang onto a situation far beyond its time.

Letting go is so hard to do but it is necessary. We have a lesson

to be learned and the ability to know when to let go is a part of

that lesson. When you are having difficulty with letting go of a

situation try this:

In your mind, imagine writing a few words about the situation

on a small piece of paper. Fold it up and put it into a bottle.

Put a cork in the bottle. Imagine walking quickly to a river that

has a bend in it and throw the bottle in. Watch it carefully

until it disappears around the bend.When it is gone from

sight, feel yourself physically let go of whatever you wrote on

the paper. Do this until you **KNOW** that you have let go.

Today I begin to let go.

ONE WITH THE ALL

We are all parts of God and he of us. Each part is necessary to make a perfect whole. We will not find our way back to the whole until we also help others to find their way.

KNOW that you are One with the All that there is. Recognize that connection now, it is a part of your soul's knowledge, bring it into your conscious awareness.

Today I recognize my connection to all souls

SPIRIT FRIENDS

Spirit friends are always with us whether or not we are able to experience their presence. Reach out your hand and it will be touched.

You may not feel it but rest assured that it is touched. They are always with us, gently guiding us from the Other Side.

They do what they do for us out of their great love.

I thank my spirit friends for their love.

CREATION

Go outside and look at a blade of grass. Study it carefully.
Handle it gently. It is a part of the Oneness just as you are,
only it doesn't have your conscious awareness of it. Stroke it
with love, tell it that you love it. Thank it for its gift of beauty
to you. Become aware of its place in the creation of the
universe. Be aware that you are also a creation of the same
universe.

I am one with all creation.

FULFILLMENT OF THE LAW

LOVE

is the fulfillment of the law.

Today I fulfill the law.

SELF LOVE

Love who you are right now without any conditions or reservations. Step outside yourself and see yourself as you really are. Then love that person right now exactly as he or she is. You are beautiful, inside and out. You are a light that reflects the love within. You are special, unique, one of a kind. There is not another exactly like you.

LOVE THIS SELF THAT YOU ARE.

TODAY I REJOICE IN THE BEING THAT IS ME.

LIFE

LIFE IS TO BE LIVED.

ENJOY IT!!

CHILDREN ARE SEPARATE SOULS

Children are separate souls. They DO NOT belong to their parents. The parents have chosen to take responsibility for the needs of the children only until they are old enough to care for themselves. Love your children but do not possess them. They are not "things" to be owned. Recognize that they are a part of the Oneness just as you are.

Today I see my children as separate souls.

MENTAL PICTURES

You can imagine mental pictures in your mind that will create your reality.

The more detailed the pictures are, the more you create.

Visualize something that you want in your life. A new job, a wonderful relationship, a move to another place, anything that you want.

Then see yourself as already having it. Play it over and over in your mind until it becomes reality.

I create a mental picture of what I really want.

OPEN TO YOUR INTUITION

The best way to open to your intuition is to listen to it. Intuition is the ability to know without words. We know but we don't know HOW we know. Learn to trust your intuition and then to follow it up with appropriate action. Learn to trust by testing it. Once you become aware that your intuition will not fail you, you will use it constantly.

Today I listen to my inner urges.

PATIENCE

One of the major lessons to be learned in life is that of patience. To gain harmony and understanding we must have patience. How do we acquire it? By applying it in every situation where it is needed. Know that NOW is the time to be patient. EVERY MOMENT is the time to be patient.

Be aware that all waiting eventually ends.

Today I exercise patience.

BALANCE

Every action has a reaction. Your reaction creates your inner balance. You are always involved in maintaining your balance. Balance is moderation in all things, not going to an extreme in anything. Only you can create the balance that is perfect for yourself. Dividing time equally between work and play may create balance for some. Giving the family first priority may create balance for others.

When you become aware that the scales of balance are tipped in one direction, go into your higher self and discover what it is that you need to do in order to bring them back into balance.

Today I check out my balance.

SHADOWS IN YOUR LIFE

Be willing to accept the shadows that occur in your life for this
is not a perfect world. That is why we are here in this imperfect
place, to learn from the shadows.

To love them, and to accept them as a part of our very being.
Also know that many of your shadows are caused by standing
in your own sunshine. Accept the responsibility for them,
learn from them and go on.

I accept the shadows in my life today.

EMOTIONS

We are here on Earth to experience the full range of emotions. Do not fear your emotions but take them into the essence of your being and feel them fully. Learn to recognize which of your emotions are based on fear. **KNOW** that there is nothing in the universe to fear and release these emotions.

LET THEM GO WITH LOVE AND GRATITUDE FOR THE LESSONS THEY HAVE TAUGHT YOU.

I allow myself to feel my full emotions.

POSITIVE THOUGHTS

Our positive thoughts feed other people. When we can accept others exactly as they are with all their flaws, we are able to control our thoughts and send out positive ones.

These positive thoughts will dissolve the negative thoughts of others and will change them. Send out positive thoughts and the world will change positively.

TRY IT.

Today I send out only positive thoughts.

PLANET EARTH

How do you view this planet that we live on? Is it something to be used without thought of giving something back? Or do you view it with love? And with the knowledge that it is a part of the Oneness just as you are? Take the time today to say thank you to the planet and resolve to treat it with the same loving care you give to others.

I take a good look at Earth today.

SOLITUDE

Do not fear solitude for it is in solitude that you discover your true self. Solitude is a source of joy. It is in solitude that you find the true meaning of the universe. Insights do not usually come when you are in a crowd of people but when you are alone. Solitude is necessary to keep our lives in balance.

I enjoy being alone.

SEEING THE LIGHT IN OTHERS

The light is within each of us but sometimes it is very hard for us to see the light in others. We must try and keep on trying. Just knowing that the light is there is a start. We must get beyond the masks that others wear to be able to see the light. When you are having a difficult situation with someone, become aware of it, stop for a moment and go inward. Feel your own light and know that the other person also has that light within them. Feel the connection:

LIGHT TO LIGHT

LOVE TO LOVE.

Today I see the light in others.

LOVE IS ALL THERE IS

The universe is made up of love. It exists. LOVE IS. It cannot be defined. All else is illusion. Think about this. Think carefully. Then put your ego aside and concentrate on universal love. You can feel it in your soul, bring it out and feel it in your body and act on it. Let it become a part of everything you do. Love lasts forever. It is what holds the universe together.

Today I know that love is all there is.

HAVE FUN

When was the last time you had fun? If you can't answer truthfully "today", you need to rethink your priorities. Fun is good for the soul as well as the body. It opens to the light and keeps things in balance.

Include having fun in your daily list of activities.

TAKE THE TIME TO HAVE FUN DAILY.

Today I do something just for the fun of it.

BE-ING

BE

AGE

Since we are all eternal, what does age matter? **KNOW** that it doesn't. We are all on different levels in our personal growth. We develop at our own pace. There is no hurry. We have eternity to learn the lessons that we need to learn.

Celebrate every year that passes as a sign of spiritual growth.

I KNOW THAT I AM ETERNAL.

GUARDIAN ANGELS

We all have Guardian Angels whether we call them by that name or not. These are spirits who assist souls who take on a physical body but they have never been in a physical body the selves. They help humans to reach their higher selves during meditation, dreams and through intuition. Their purpose is to watch over us and remind us to always choose the spiritual path.

Today I thank my Guardian Angels for their guidance.

GIVE OF YOURSELF

There is one gift that we can all give to others regardless of our circumstances in life. That is the gift of ourselves. We can give our time, effort and energy to be of service to others.
Sometimes a silent hug can help more than a thousand words. Let people know that you recognize the loving connection that joins each of us to the Oneness.

Today I give of myself.

UNIVERSAL TRUTH #2

The more you give out to the universe, the more you will receive. The more you are of service to others, the more you help yourself. The more love you give out, the more love you receive.

KNOW THIS TRUTH.

I recognize this truth in the essence of my being.

BEAUTY

Beauty is everywhere. Look around you. See it. It is your choice whether or not you see beauty.

Open yourself up and allow the beauty to enter you.

BEAUTY IS JOY.

BEAUTY IS PEACE.

BEAUTY IS LOVE.

I see beauty everywhere.

CHOOSING A SYMBOL

Choose a symbol that represents peace to you. It could be a mountain, a lake, tree, moon, flower, bird, animal or anything that feels appropriate to you. Concentrate on that symbol, fill it with peace. Whenever you are feeling anxious, or uncomfortable in any way, stop a moment and feel your symbol. Close your eyes, go inside yourself and feel the peace as it enters your body and quiets your mind. Allow it to do so.

Today I choose a peace symbol.

CREATING YOUR OWN JOY

Stop right now and say these words aloud: I AM JOYFUL. Put expression and feeling in your voice as you speak. Say the words as many times as is necessary until the feeling is actually there. NOW: FEEL THE FEELING! Doesn't it feel wonderful! Do this every time you are lacking joy in your life.

**I AM JOYFUL! I AM JOYFUL!
I AM JOYFUL! I AM JOYFUL!**

DEATH

The acceptance of our own death brings with it the freedom to really live. We don't care so much about the things we thought mattered before. We can see them for what they are steps in our spiritual growth. Death is the closing of one door and the opening of another. Knowing this, we can use our energy to live life to the fullest.

Today I begin to accept my own death.

LIGHTING UP THE UNIVERSE

TOGETHER

ALL SOULS LIGHT UP THE UNIVERSE.

LIKE ATTRACTS LIKE

Give to others what you want to receive. Give love, support, healing, appreciation, acknowledgement and forgiveness. It will return to you many times over. Giving empowers you to see yourself in a more loving way. You will love and support yourself as you do it for others. Become the peace, harmony and love that you want to attract.

Today I give to others what I want to receive myself.

RECEIVING

Allow others to be of service to you. It is a tender act of caring. It is just as important to receive as it is to give. It is a growth experience to be of service to others. Do not let pride and love of independence keep you from accepting the offer of a person to be of service. Give yourself the opportunity of being loving to another by allowing him to be of service to you.

I am willing to receive.

ILLUSION

The physical world that we live in is nothing but dream, an illusion. Our bodies are also an illusion.

Death is the great illusion.

KNOW THIS:

We never die, we are only transformed. Illusions are thoughts that become games that we create in order to learn what we need to learn for our personal growth.

Today I recognize the physical world as an illusion.

ONENESS #2

ALL ENERGY IS ONE.

WE ARE ALL ENERGY.

HENCE

WE ARE ALL ONE.

ALTERING YOUR VIEWPOINT

The way that you look at things colors everything you experience. This can be changed by a positive effort. If you are unable to view things as beautiful make a concentrated effort to view them as neutral.

Try this experiment:

Take a situation in your life that isn't working and mentally change the way you look at it. You do not have to do anything else. Whenever this situation enters your mind and disturbs you, stop and change the thought from negative to positive or neutral. Do this faithfully for two weeks and see if your viewpoint doesn't change.

Today I begin to change my viewpoint on something in my life that isn't working.

GUILT

Acknowledge your guilt, resolve not to let it happen again and let it go. That's all you have to do.

There is no need to beat yourself up over it.

Guilt is a waste of good energy.

Do not allow anyone to make you feel guilty.

They are only trying to control you or hurt you.

Become aware when others are trying to manipulate you by guilt tactics.

Respond with love towards them as well as yourself.

I let go of all guilt feelings.

SELF LOVE #2

People who love themselves are generous and kind to others as well as themselves.

They trust themselves and know who they are and they act on that trust.

Look into a mirror. Look deep into your eyes, feel the love you see there. Express it out loud. Say, "I love the being I see in the mirror. It is me and I love me just as I am."

I love myself.

LOVING LIFE

Choose to love life. You have that choice. Whatever the circumstances that surround you, you can choose to love life. Choosing to love is also choosing to reject fear and frustration. Let your channels be wide open so that the joy can flow through you and out into the universe where it can benefit others as well as yourself.

Today I love living.

SUNSHINE IN YOUR HEART

Is the sun shining outside? Is it shining in your heart? If not, why not? Open up your heart and let the sun shine in. It is only waiting for you to open and allow it to enter.

Do so now. Feel its light, feel the warmth as it fills your heart and travels throughout your body. Allow this to happen. You can do it. Let it fill you with its golden glow, then take that golden glow and give it to someone else.

Today I let the sun shine in my heart.

THE ANSWER TO EVERY PROBLEM

The answer to every problem is found within you. It is there, complete in every way.

It is only waiting for you to bring it into your consciousness.

When you think that you don't know how to solve a problem, quiet your mind and seek the solution within.

Then let it go and forget about it until the answer comes to you. Don't have any expectations of how the answer comes.

Know only that it will come.

Trust the wisdom of your inner self.

I seek answers within.

CONTENTMENT

What makes you content? Stop a moment and think carefully about this. Now answer these two questions:

1) How long can you be utterly content before you begin to feel uncomfortable?

2) Are you aware of the limits you put on yourself?

Realize exactly what your feelings consist of when you feel more contentment than usual. Use these feelings to help you increase the contentment in your life.

I increase my contentment by realizing what makes me content.

KNOW YOURSELF

Take the time to get to know yourself. You are a wondrous being. Go inside and get to know you. Accept yourself in all its different parts. Love it just as it is. Once you do that you can take the appropriate action to change any part that you wish.

I KNOW WHO I AM

SURRENDER #1

Say the word "surrender" out loud. Where do you feel it? In your heart area, your solar plexus or your lower abdomen? Or where? Say it again. How does it make you feel? Keep saying it until you understand what the feeling FEELS like. Do you feel that you have lost control?

Or do you feel that you no longer NEED to control but can safely allow things to flow as they will and you flow with them?

I examine what surrender means to me.

LOOKING OUT THE WINDOW

Right now, where ever you are, go to a window and look out.
What do you see? Buildings, streets, houses, cars, sidewalks,
TV antennas, fences, what? Look at each thing very carefully
and say thank you to it for its gift of being. Everything that you
see is a creation which originated in the thoughts of someone.
Those houses, cars, sidewalks were all ideas in the mind of
man at one time. Now they have come into being. Isn't that
marvelous!

Think about it.

Today I see the wonder of MAN'S creation.

BEHOLD GOD

Look in a mirror. BEHOLD GOD.

OPENING YOUR HEART

The heart will open just as a rose opens, petal by petal. If too much pain enters, it will close again. Being willing to receive from others as well as the universe causes the heart to open. Loving and giving to others also opens the heart. The desire to open the heart is enough to unfold the petals. Resolve now to open your heart and let the light of love enter.

Today I open my heart.

AWARENESS

Take a deep breath, relax and become aware of everything that is occurring around you. Listen and feel. Hear the tick of the clock, the bird sing, the voices of the children outside. Feel your heart beating, the blood going through your veins. Acknowledge the fact that you are a part of everything around you and within you and that everything is a part of you.

Feel the Oneness, the connection.

Become aware of what is going on inside you.

Today I am aware of what is inside of me and outside of me.

FEAR #2

Become aware of when fear is present in your life. Become still and go into your heart. Experience what is going on there without judgment. Be an observer to your feelings of fear. Realize that the center of your heart is where your love is and where the fear will fade away if you will allow it to do so. Feel the love that connects you to everything and ever one.

I AM SAFE.

PERFECT PEACE

I CHOOSE TO SPEND THIS DAY IN PERFECT PEACE. I WILL NOT ALLOW ANYTHING OR ANYONE TO DISTURB THIS PEACE. THIS PEACE COMES FROM AN INNER KNOWLEDGE THAT I HAVE NOTHING TO FEAR, THAT I AM LOVE AND LIGHT AND THAT I AM A PART OF THE ONENESS.
THIS PERFECT PEACE SHINES THROUGH ME AND AFFECTS EVERYONE THAT I MEET.

SO BE IT!!!

I SPEND THIS DAY IN PERFECT PEACE.

RESISTANCE TO CHANGE

We cannot change until we first become aware of our resistance to change. Patterns of behavior have existed in us for a long, long time. First, we must allow the condition to rise to the surface. Then we must study it to see why we are resisting changing it. Become aware that you created the behavior-condition-situation and take full responsibility for it. Give up the resistance and learn what it is you need to learn in order to change.

Today I pay attention to my resistance to change.

QUIET YOUR MIND

Make time each day to quiet your mind. It takes practice but you can do it. Take a few minutes daily to make your mind still. When a thought crosses your mind, brush it aside without any pressure and breathe deeply. When your mind is quiet you are fully present and recognize that now is all there is. You become aware of the peace and love within you and outside of you.

I take three minutes today to quiet my mind.

BEING A TEACHER

Each of us is a teacher as well as a student in the experience called life. As we are learning we are also teaching by the way we live our lives. Everything we truly learn we incorporate into our life style. Become aware of what you are teaching others. If it isn't appropriate to what you truly know, change it.

I become aware that I am teaching others by my actions.

SELF LOVE #3

When you love yourself, you are able to receive as well as to give. You receive with joy, knowing that you are not taking anything away from anyone else, but actually adding to them. There is plenty of everything for everyone in the universe. Find pleasure in everything that you do and glory in it because of the love you feel for yourself and others.

I love others as I love myself.

FRIENDSHIP

What does friendship mean to you? Is a friend someone to talk with when you are depressed? Someone to enjoy activities with? Someone to lend you money? Friendship is a feeling that comes directly from the heart. It is the recognition of one soul for another. It is the recognition of the connection between all of us. Friendship is love on a soul level brought to the surface.

Today I am a friend.

DOUBT

Since we are not perfect beings we will carry doubt
with us in this lifetime. It is all right. IT IS ALL RIGHT. We
will still learn the lessons we need to learn even if we doubt.
Take the doubt into your heart and love it because it is a part
of you. Don't let the doubt incapacitate you but overcome it.

I accept my doubts.

BASEBALL

The game of baseball is like the game of life:

IT IS THE COMING HOME THAT COUNTS.

NO SHORTCUTS

There are no shortcuts to wisdom, to knowledge or to understanding. Every soul must live these experiences until. they become a part of the essence of the soul. They must be experienced over and over again. Sometimes we try to take a shortcut to get to the journey's end quicker but the shortcut turns out to be a main path that teaches us the lesson that we need to learn.

There are no shortcuts in life.

RAINBOWS

When you see a rainbow, you feel a sense of wonder. An inner knowledge that everything is all right. Visualize a rainbow in your mind when you become fearful or filled with stress. See the rainbow clearly and feel the comfort and peace that it brings you. Take a deep breath, smile, and know that the rainbow is your sign that everything is all right.

I see rainbows in my life.

THE STILL SMALL VOICE

Be still and listen to the still small voice that comes from the deepest center of your being.

The outside world cannot enter into this part of you.

Quiet your mind and listen carefully to the whisper of the still small voice.

It speaks of harmony, peace, love and wholeness.

BE STILL AND LISTEN

THERE IS ONLY NOW

This minute, this very second, is all that counts. There is only NOW. No yesterday, no tomorrow, only now. Value it, love it, use it to the best of your ability. Every moment has energy, it is alive, it creates. USE IT. It is all there is. Fill it with love and joy.

I live in the now.

SHARING JOY

Resolve that, just for today, you will share the joy that you feel with every person that you meet. That person's day will be happier just because you had a small part in it. A smile, a kind word of encouragement, a pat on the back, a compliment. Each of these small gifts will help you to spread your joy around.

I smile joyfully at each person I see today.

ACCEPTANCE #2

Now that you have accepted yourself exactly as you are, it's time to accept others in the same way. Let go of any expectations, judgments and desires to change them. See them EXACTLY as they are and accept them. Work at this, without putting any pressure on yourself, until it becomes automatic. Feel the sense of freedom acceptance gives you. Isn't it glorious!

I accept others exactly as they are.

TAKE OFF YOUR MASK

Each of us spends a great deal of time hiding behind a variety of masks. We hide our innermost thoughts and desires from others. We wear the masks that we think society forces us to wear because we are afraid of not receiving approval if we take them off and reveal our true selves. Thus, we let outward forces control us rather than taking control ourselves.

Have the courage to take off your mask and reveal yourself exactly as you are.

Today I take off my mask.

DO WHAT YOU LOVE

What gives you the most satisfaction in life?

Take some time to figure it out and when you are sure

DO IT.

Don't let anyone or anything stop you.

DO WHAT YOU LOVE.

FEAR OF THE UNKNOWN

There is nothing truly unknown in the universe, only temporarily unknown. Our souls have already experienced all things. We have forgotten that and we are here on the Earth plane to remember it. Be comforted and **KNOW** that everything that happens will help to make us more aware of the growth of our soul. There is nothing to fear, there is nothing truly unknown.

Today I look into the unknown with love.

GETTING INVOLVED IN LIFE

Become truly involved in life by being of service to others.

Don't be afraid that you will be hurt if you get involved.

We are here to experience all things. Lend a helping hand where ever it is needed.

Do it gently, tenderly, with great love and compassion and without thought of anything in return.

Today I become truly involved in life.

TRUST YOURSELF

To trust yourself means that you allow whatever is inside you to come to the outside and you accept it as it is without any judgments. It also means learning from every experience that occurs in your life. Trusting yourself means learning to enjoy all that you are. Trust yourself to know whether or not you are coming from your heart.

I TRUST MYSELF

SURRENDER #2

Put aside the need to know what is going to happen in the future and leave your heart open.

Trust that the universe will lead you to the place that proves most beneficial to you at that time.

Trust that you are being guided always.

Accept that guidance with gratitude and love.

I release my need to know about the future.

DREAMS

Do you remember your: dreams? Do you pay attention to them? Dreams are symbols that need to be interpreted. They can tell us many things about ourselves and the way we live. They are like looking at an abstract painting and describing what that painting says to us. Our higher self often speaks to us in dreams. We need to learn what our dreams are telling us and apply it in our daily life.

I am learning to pay attention to my dreams.

EXAMINE YOUR LIFE

Study your life carefully and see where you are not using your energy appropriately. Write these areas down on a piece of paper. Work on one area at a time until you have changed it into a loving energy. Soon your whole life will be working just the way you want it.

Trust yourself enough to make the necessary changes.

I begin examining my life today.

CREATING YOUR OWN REALITY

Everything that is created begins as a thought or idea. If you are not satisfied with your reality as you perceive it, you can change it by changing your thoughts. The creative power of your mind is unlimited. Become aware of the thousands of thoughts that enter your mind daily. Then decide what you want to change and begin by changing your thoughts.

Today I pay attention to ALL the thoughts that enter my mind.

ALONENESS

Being alone is not the same as being lonely. Being alone allows you to be all that you can be. You have the opportunity to learn to know yourself. Spend some time alone each day getting to know the wonderful being that is you. Explore your inner self, then bring it out for others to enjoy with you.

Today I spend time getting to know myself.

RESPONSIBILITY

YOU are the only one responsible for your life. No one else. YOU are NOT responsible for anyone else's life. You only have to take care of your own life and let everyone else take care of theirs. This knowledge will give you a sense of freedom.

Use this freedom wisely to benefit others as well as yourself.

Today I take responsibility for my thoughts and actions.

EXPECTATIONS

NEVER EXPECT ANYTHING FROM ANYONE.

RELEASE YOUR EXPECTATIONS AND ACCEPT TOTALLY.

I let go of all expectations

SHARING JOY #2

There are so many people who do not seem to have any joy of their own. Bring your joy to the surface and share it with them. Do it out of love, with the awareness that you are all a part of the Oneness. Let them know that it comes from the heart of you which is pure love.

I share my joy out of love.

STAR GAZING

Go outside tonight and look at the stars. See their beauty and majesty. Marvel at the wonder of them. Say thank you to them for their light and beauty. Carry their beauty and light with you wherever you go. Choose one star and visit it every night.

FEEL THE CONNECTION BETWEEN ITS LIGHT AND YOURS.

Tonight, I gaze at the stars.

TOUCHING

Touching does not always consist of physical contact. You touch others when you think of them with love. Each loving thought that you send out touches the person and affects them. Take the time today to touch someone who is a far distance from you.

Send them love.

Today I touch someone far away.

FORGIVENESS

There is no need for forgiveness when there is total acceptance. However, since we are human and live in an imperfect world, the need still exists for forgiveness for ourselves and others. Examine your life. Is there someone that you are not forgiving? Why not? Let the bitterness go and forgive. Forgiveness is the same as letting go. **KNOW** that everything happens in order to teach us lessons about ourselves and our lives. Forgiveness begins in the heart.

It takes courage to look within, to forgive and to change.

Today I have the courage to forgive.

TRUSTING THE UNIVERSE

Trust the universe to support you spiritually, emotionally, financially and in any other way that you need it. It takes courage to trust and to give up control. Trusting the universe will take you to the experiences that you need to learn for your soul's growth.

GO WITH THE FLOW

I trust the universe.

ATONEMENT

AT-ONE-MENT

UNIVERSAL LANGUAGE

The only universal language is LOVE.

SPEAK IT TODAY.

Today I speak _only_ the universal language.

TRUTH

Truth is the actual essence of the universe.

Truth is the way creation is expressed in man and nature.

Truth is your power and your freedom.

TRUTH IS

ON TOP OF THE MOUNTAIN

Remember when you were a child and played "King of the

Hill"? It was a glorious and exciting feeling, wasn't it?

Pretend now that you are on top of a mountain.

Feel the majesty of the mighty mountain and enjoy its beauty.

Know that you are king of everything you see. Feel the wonder
and awe throughout your whole body.

When you come down, carry the feeling with you into the
everyday world.

Hold on to it as long as you can.

Today I carry with me the majesty of the mountain.

DEATH #2

Death is nothing to fear. Even when you are "dead" you are still alive. The reason that we fear death is that we fear the step into the unknown. IT'S ALL RIGHT. Love the part of you that is afraid.

KNOW that you are safe.

Death is an illusion. We never die, we go through another door where life and consciousness continue. Beyond the door is the light, brighter and more beautiful than you have ever seen it.

The light is peace and love.

I realize that death is light.

STRANGERS

THERE ARE NO STRANGERS.

Only friends we do not know.

KNOW this:

On a soul level we all recognize one another as part of the whole.

It is only on the surface that we are not aware of this fact. Open yourself up and allow the light from "strangers" to enter.

Love the stranger

I realize that we are all a part of the whole.

UNCONDITIONAL LOVE

Unconditional love is NOT what is commonly referred to as "romantic love."

Unconditional love means to love without conditions, limits, expectations or judgments.

It means to ACCEPT others exactly as they are and still love them.

It means we do not try to change anyone but ourselves.

It means rising above emotions that are based on fear and it means living and expressing only love.

It begins with the self because you cannot love anyone else until you first love yourself.

Today I love myself unconditionally.

THE CHILD WITHIN

There is a child within each of us struggling to get out. LET IT OUT. It is the part of you that loves to play. Playing is fun, do it as often as you want.

Giggle with joy as you swing or slide or jump rope.

Enjoy the respite from being an adult.

These simple joys will refresh and balance you.

Today I let the child in me out.

ONE WITH THE ALL #2

There is a longing within each soul to return to its source. We are all a part of that original creation and we yearn to be made whole again. Recognize that yearning within yourself. Stop and listen to it. Feel it with every part of your being. Know that you are One with the All yet, by yourself, you are not that All.

I know that I am One with the All.

UNSEEN INFLUENCES

Are you aware of how telepathic messages and emotions sent from others affect you?

Whenever someone thinks of you, that thought, whether positive or not, has an effect on you.

That thought or emotion is energy and has the power to influence you.

Be sure to send out only positive thoughts and emotions for you will draw back to you what you send out.

Today I pay attention to the influences others have on me.

ENDURANCE

YOU DO NOT HAVE TO ENDURE ANYTHING.

ALL YOU HAVE TO DO IS TAKE WHAT YOU THINK YOU MUST ENDURE INTO YOUR ESSENCE AND LOVE IT.

VIBRATIONS

The universe is made up of matter which is energy. Energy cannot stand still, it must move. The movement is vibration. The vibrational rate of each person is determined by the thoughts and feelings that he has experienced in the past and is experiencing in the present.

When we act in harmony and in service with ourselves and others we raise our vibrational rates.

Today I make a conscious effort to raise my vibrational rate.

YOUR BODY

Starting right now, LOVE YOUR BODY. You have criticized and judged it for years. Now show your body that you love and respect it. Take care of it, say thank you to it for the years of good service that it has given you. As you learn to love your body it will feel lighter and filled with energy. You will glow with love and it will show.

I love my body without judgment.

SUFFERING

God DID NOT create suffering. You don't need to suffer. You are here to learn to experience life and to grow from the experience. Choose not to suffer but to see everything as growth. See the long-range view. You are on earth for such a short time that you can easily overcome all obstacles if you choose to do so. Suffering is useless. It helps no one or anything.

You do NOT have to go through pain and suffering in order to grow.

Wisdom erases suffering.

I choose not to suffer.

LAUGHTER

When you are laughing you are open to the light. You allow the light to enter you and flow through you to others around you. Laughter is good for the soul as well as the physical body. Share a heartfelt laugh with someone today.

I laugh with joy today.

BE LIKE THE WIND

The wind can be a strong force that can move the impossible yet it can also be a warm gentle breeze. You do not have to stand against it but surrender to it and become a part of it.

Be like the wind, for it is a part of you and you are a part of it.

I recognize my connection to the wind.

TIME

Past, present, future. That's the way we view time. Yet there is no past, no future, there is only the present. Babies have no concept of time, they relate only to the present. It's only as we grow older that time becomes a factor. Time is a measurement that we use for our growth.

It is a tool for use in the schoolroom of life.

As we learn we recognize time as consciousness.

I live only in the present.

FEAR #3

The power of love is always much stronger than the power of fear. Fear is an illusion, it is not real. Rest and be comforted in the awareness that you are a glorious part of the eternal light and that you need never fear anything or anyone.

YOU ARE SAFE.

YOU ARE SAFE.

YOU ARE SAFE.

I am safe.

THERE/HERE

Did you ever realize that if you take the "T" away from THERE you have HERE?

Today I recognize that I am HERE.

TRANSFORMATION

Do not fear transformation. Be gentle with yourself as you discover your reluctance to let go of the old and become the new. Even when you know that you need to let go of your old self, it is difficult to take that next step into the unknown. Transformation comes through self-acceptance.

DO NOT FEAR.

REMEMBER THE BUTTERFLY

Today I am transformed.

YOUR OWN LITTLE WORLD

We each have our own little worlds where we feel secure.

But **KNOW** this:

We are all connected to everything in the universe.

Become fully aware of this fact.

KNOW it in every part of your being.

Open up your world and let others in.

Do not be afraid to broaden your horizon.

Leave your world and go out into the universe.

KNOW that we are all the same underneath.

It is only on the outside that we appear to have differences.

Fill your own little world with love and then send it out into the universe.

Today I dissolve the boundaries of my world.

WORDS

THERE ARE NO IDLE WORDS.

We have a special ability to choose our own words and to speak them as we will.

We are the only creatures on Earth who have this ability.

We have the power to create with our words.

Our words also have a strong effect on the attitudes and feelings of those who listen.

Words can be a source of wisdom and comfort.

Be careful to only choose words that inspire and uplift.

Today I am careful about the words I say.

POTHOLES

As you travel the road of life you will discover many potholes in your path.

Do not let them discourage you but go THROUGH them slowly, gently, and with great love.

They are there to help you with the lessons that you need to learn.

I love the potholes in my life.

PLAYING

What's your favorite way of playing?

You have one, what is it? How long since you've done it?

What keeps you from doing it more often?

Let the child in you out.

 Feel the delight that you receive from playing.

Throw your whole self into the playing.

Doesn't it make you feel really alive?

Don't you feel the connection between you and the universe? Enjoy it! Go on!

Don't take yourself so seriously, life is fun!

Today I take the time to play.

UNLIMITED FREEDOM

You have the unlimited freedom to be, to become and to express through your actions whatever you desire to be. You know this in your inner being, bring it into your conscious awareness and act on it. You can create for yourself whatever you want to become. That freedom is yours.

Today I recognize my unlimited freedom.

ONENESS #3

ONENESS IS LOVE.

PHYSICAL HEALING

Physical healing can only be accomplished when there is spiritual healing. Your illness is a message from your soul telling you to listen to what your body is saying. Ask your body to explain to you and listen carefully to the answer. You can learn from the pain. Take it into yourself and change the energy. The body reacts to the soul. If you learn the lesson the pain is telling you to learn, you will realize that the pain wasn't important after all.

I realize all physical pain comes from the soul in order to teach us a needed lesson.

SURRENDER #3

Surrender is a matter of trust and acceptance of the Oneness. Let go of your ego-self and become willing to accept this truth with sincerity and a open heart. Simply know that there is a higher power guiding you always. Use your free will to yield your life to that guidance.

I let go of all control and simply trust.

PUT MORE HUMOR IN YOUR LIFE

Start a scrapbook of cartoons, comic strips, greeting cards, funny signs, jokes and anything else that you find funny. Keep it up to date and take it out and look at it every time that you need a good laugh.

Laughter is very good for the soul as it opens you up and allows the light to enter. Humor is also a great relaxer for the physical body.

Today I begin collecting items for my scrapbook.

THERE ARE NO ACCIDENTS

This is hard to understand, isn't it?

KNOW THIS:

Your emotions, your thoughts, your words and your actions **CAUSE** all your experiences. All of us together, create the environment we live in. Everything, before it came into being, was first an idea in someone's mind. When the majority of people focus their attention on a certain type of energy, that energy creates.

I recognize that there are no accidents in life.

CONNECTING TO THE EARTH

We are all a part of the Earth and it is part of us. All things are connected. We need to recognizethat the Earth does not belong to us. There are energy vortexes on Earth that give off power to help people with their lives. If you allow the Earth to nourish you, you will not demand nourishment from others. Give to the Earth and it will give to you.

I feel my connection to Earth.

LOOKING GOOD

Looking good has nothing to do with how you dress or wear your hair or how much you weigh. It has everything to do with how you feel in your heart. If you love yourself, the beauty of it will shine through you and appear on the outside. Everyone around you will feel the radiance of your light.

Today I look good on the outside because I feel good on the inside.

JOY IN THE MIDST OF TROUBLE

When circumstances are the worst in our lives is when we need to realize that WE ARE LIGHT, that we aren't alone, that we are a part of the Oneness. This awareness will help us to lift up our heads and shout joyfully. We know that we are love and love is all there is. We become aware that our troubles are providing us with a great opportunity to learn and grow. We know that we are eternal and nothing can ever change that.

We let the joy out.

I feel the joy in the midst of trouble.

WALKING IN ANOTHER'S SHOES

If you have compassion for others you will be able to put yourself in their shoes and see things from their point of view.

Is there someone in your life that you are struggling with?

Put yourself in his or her place and see yourself as he or she sees you.

Go into your heart and become aware of the love and compassion there.

Recognize all the pain and suffering that person has gone through. Understand why they feel the way they do.

Then let go of any hurt and resentment you still feel.

KNOW that they are love just as you are.

Recognize the connection between you.

Today I walk in another's shoes.

WISDOM

Everything that happens is an experience to learn wisdom. If you have the wisdom to learn your lessons through love and positive action, there will be no suffering. The wiser you become, the more understanding you become, not only of yourself but of everyone else.

Wisdom and love walk hand in hand.

Today I recognize my need for wisdom.

YOUR IDEAL DAY

Take a piece of paper and write down your ideal day, hour by hour. What kind of work would you like to be doing? What kind of dwelling do you want to live in? What kind of relationships would you like to have? What would you do for fun? How would you share your joy? Would you take the time to commune with your higher self?

Refine your ideal day until it is exactly how you want it to be.

THEN CREATE IT!

My ideal day includes spiritual nourishment.

THE JOY OF EATING

Eating is a pleasure, don't ever forget that. Really taste your food today. Think about it as you eat it and enjoy, enjoy, enjoy!

Say thank you to your food for its gift to you.

Recognize the joy that comes from the taste of good food.

Today I enjoy my food.

WHAT'S NEXT

Once you have completed a project you often find yourself wondering, "what' s next"? Rest assured that there is always something else to begin and to complete. Do not fear the sense of emptiness that often accompanies the completion of something. There is always more to learn and to do. Look towards it with joy and eagerness.

Today I begin something new.

WHOLENESS

We are all a part of the whole.

What one does affects the whole.

KNOW THIS TO BE TRUTH.

Be careful that the energy you send out into the wholeness is either positive or neutral. Wholeness is you and me, together, without any separation. We are complete, we are love.

I recognize that I am a part of the whole.

SURRENDER #4

THE LAST STEP TO TRUE SURRENDER IS

TO LET GO OF THE DESIRE TO SURRENDER.

REMEMBER WHO YOU ARE

Look in the mirror again.

*REMEMBER WHO YOU ARE**

*See page 74

UNIVERSAL LOVE

There is enough love in the universe for everyone. It can never be used up. Love is all there is. Love DOES make the world go around. Universal love begins with self-love and then goes on to encompass everything and everyone. There is no limit to how much love you can experience and give out. Allow yourself to experience this love.

It is all around you.

Today I experience universal love.

www.ingramcontent.com/pod-product-compliance
Lightning Source LLC
Chambersburg PA
CBHW060255050426
42448CB00009B/1648